STREET CALLIGRAPHY

STREET CALLIGRAPHY

Poems by Jim Daniels

ISBN: 978-0-9863575-3-4

Book design by Chad Christensen

Published by STEEL TOE BOOKS
steeltoebooks.com

Steel Toe Books
Western Kentucky University
Department of English
1906 College Heights Blvd. #11086
Bowling Green, KY 42101-1086

Steel Toe Books is affiliated with Western Kentucky University

ACKNOWLEDGMENTS

The Alembic: "Hair on Fire"
Artful Dodge: "Slow Learner"
Blue Mesa Review: "Grilled Cheese at the Rehab Center"
Bloodroot: "The Macular Degeneration Boogie"
Briar Cliff Review: "Nevertheless"
Chelsea: "First Communion"
Cimarron Review: "Caucus of My Great Fall"
Crab Orchard Review: "The Wave, Tiger Stadium"
Ducts: "Last Meals"
Fail Better: "Turning Down the Ars Poetica, Heating Up the Leftovers"
Fat City Review: "Posted Limits"
Gargoyle: "Spinning Donuts in Universal City Mall Parking Lot"
The Georgia Review: "Street Calligraphy," "Tennis Practice Wall"
Jai-Alai: "Lazarus in the Sprinkler"
Lake Effect: "Grandfather Rents to Pimp"
The Laurel Review: "Short Guide to the Addiction Memoir"
The Mid-American Review: "Premature Aging"
Midwestern Gothic: "Story Problem"
Moon City: "Cutwoman in the Corner House"
Natural Bridge: "House of Drumming, House of Song"
The New Delta Review: "Changing the Name"
The New Ohio Review: "Up on Blocks"
Passages North: "Christmas Miracle"
The Plume Anthology, 2012: "Last Day in Coldwater"
Postcard Poems and Prose Magazine: "Addict's Guide to Fatherhood"
Prairie Schooner: "Ohio Turnpike Opens New Rest Stop," "Flight"
Slipstream: "Stagger"
Southern Humanities Review: "Dusk, July, Third Floor"
Southern Poetry Review: "Key to the Cottage," "Witnesses"
The Southern Review: "The Rusty Muffler of Nostalgia"
Subtropics: "The Names of Dinosaurs"
Superstition Review: "Crack the Whip"
Tampa Review: "Model/Father"
Third Coast: "If You Ever Have to Do This Yourself"
Toasted Cheese: "Talking About the Day"
Wake: Great Lakes Thought and Culture: "The Lincoln Death Chair"

Some of these poems also appeared in *Apology to the Moon*, a chapbook published by BatCat Press. Thanks to Kevin, Kristin, and Marc for their help with this manuscript.

CONTENTS

I.

II.

III.

IV.

I.

Turning Down the Ars Poetica, Heating Up the Leftovers

The heart abused by the staged endings
of professional wrestling and greeting cards.

The line pumping blood replaced
by fashionable stray threads leading to

the complete fraying of, spraying of, the blind horse's
nod and wink. In other words, lost in the snowy forest

among the skeleton trees, irony serves little purpose.
I just won an award for obscure clarity—stop the presses

and replace them with long underwear drying on the line,
almost sideways in March wind.

*

Somewhere, a man arrives home from working over-
time in streetlight darkness, car door etching itself

on the street's silence, Inside, leftovers on the stove.
A woman in her robe prepares his plate.

Five children asleep, radio tuned to talk
on health and home improvement and religion

though it's just soft static now as she sits
to watch him eat, as he sits to savor

what he missed. I can't tell you whether
they even hug or kiss before collapsing

into bed together, for I am already in dream's
tender arms. And if this violates point of view

or logic, she'll get you a plate
and explain it all to you, my mother.

THE RUSTY MUFFLER OF NOSTALGIA

Four teenaged boys farting in my tiny Satellite
heads hanging out the window
all the way from Detroit to Myrtle Beach.
Fun?
            I'll swear on a case of PBR longnecks
that it was. Life promised few great adventures
after Power Mechanics and Auto Shop,
after parking-lot brawls and drunk-
driving lessons.
                        So why not go full blast
into a beer-shotgunning contest? The meter
was ticking. We were wasting gas. The one fact
was fact-ory.
                  Souvenirs? Sand-burns
and hickeys from North Carolina girls. We admired
their accents. We shrugged at their high-pitched plans
for college, then kissed them some more.
                                    Nostalgia
is for suckers. I couldn't find any of those guys now.
It's not like we're going to attend

                        a reunion.
Back home playing softball, the guys razzed me
about Marsha from NC and how she sang my name
like it was ice cream on a stick. My girlfriend stopped
rooting for me—left early and alone,
and I was almost glad of it.
                        Our fathers' heavy shit
dumped in our arms as we slumped down
from the graduation stage, our bravado shrunk
by tomorrow's cold, cold water.
                        We'd watched Aaron
hit 715 on the motel TV and cheered sullenly at somebody

doing something greater than anybody else. We didn't give
a damn about The Babe. After watching the moon landing
years earlier, we shrugged, then went outside to explode
firecrackers. Why land on the moon
                                        just to walk around
surrounded by nothing? They needed some rock 'n' roll
up there. In the tiny universe of my old Plymouth Satellite,
AM only, sometimes we could tune in a loud guitar
and make it louder. We were a speck rattling down I-75
with the other specks, ants in search of honey
when we were both
                          ants and honey. This is true, though
I lied about nostalgia. It's draping itself over my shoulders
like the cape on James Brown as he left the stage—thrown off
and returned, thrown off, returned, till James finally left
and didn't come back. I don't know how many times
I'll start to leave, a phone full of dead numbers and people.
"I remember, I remember, I remember," chanted
like a used-up prayer half-memorized,
half-forgotten.
                    If someone says,
"They don't make 'em like they used to,"
ask, "How did they used to make 'em?"
Because they make them the same damn way.
Four guys in a car thinking they—well,
not thinking at all. That's the beauty of it.
The tragedy of it. That's the punch line
to the question, "What are you going to do
with the rest of your life?" We lined up in a row
and gunned beers and burped
enormous fat ellipses, like explorers
taking notes on our vanished childhoods.
We'd be lost for two more months
                                          until graduation,
then inevitably found at the factory gate. Luck
was something we kept in our wallets

like a rubber until it dried out. Luck was a concept,
like a tadpole turning into a frog and the frog
getting mistaken for a toad and the toad
                                        tossed
from a moving vehicle to see if it could fly
only to be run over by one of us on our way to work
one spring morning when we should've been
at least treading water in a pool of hope and ambition
instead of turning in our keys at the factory door
where they instructed us
                                to make more keys, different keys,
keys with no guarantees, identical keys cut with the teeth
of our fathers who stood watching us enter the gates
like bored angels guarding Limbo, like, like—okay,
give me my purple cape. I'm crawling off the stage.
Let it drag in the dust. Let it sweep up
what remains.

STREET CALLIGRAPHY

Shingles blown from roofs or spacers pried
from between concrete slabs
lasted longer than chalk but not forever.

Chalk was school. Nobody bought
chalk. Plaster worked, cracked drywall
heaped for trash. We dusted its edges
against concrete in gritty, deliberate scrawl.

What we lacked in depth
we made up for with blatant lies
or cruel wishes: *Eats Shit. Sucks Dick.*

The truth was off its hinges
or hidden in the blind spot
the world had for us, somewhere
beyond mirrors or jewelry.

Nothing harder than concrete.
Certainly not our skin. Certainly not glass.
I stashed shingles and plaster
beneath a broken brick in a field of weeds.

We marked out narrow diamonds, baselines
squeezed into the choked vein of our street.
The only fair balls shot right down the middle
then rolled and rolled, coming to rest
under parked cars or against distant curbs.

Our balls were taped or rubber, our bats plastic,
or cracked and nailed. Our mitts theoretical.
We drew football yard markers

and end zone designs. Cars served as both
obstacle and blocker. Ricochets
off windshields were ruled complete.

Leaked oil and antifreeze
marked parking spots.
The cruel whimsy of safe-T-glass
lay sprinkled against the curb
like the dice of large insects
or small rodents.

We had no tears, and nothing
with which to make tears. Don't
get me wrong, I wish we had tears.
To dilute the street, drain anger,
erase bitterness, soften the fist.

Tar blackened our fingers
tacky in summer as we drew dark lines,
stick men, designed for crude cursing,
pure permanent wobble.

We came equipped to trash
each other. Short-witted,
dim-sighted, prone to slamming
on brakes, leaving rubber lines
to be examined like near misses.

Down the empty eyes of manhole covers
we shoved our true messages—
unread in their dark falling disappearance.

I wrote, FIND ME on a scrap of paper
with a nub of bitten pencil. Alone on the curb,
I sat watching rain darken cement
till all dots connected.

It smelled like our lives then, the damp glisten
of time, the baited shove toward our futures.
Tar—tell me anything before the torn slice of roof

disintegrates into an articulate mirage. Our street,
a book permanently open to the same two pages.
Demanding to be memorized.

Tennis Practice Wall

Brick painted dull yellow once,
then abandoned to spray artists
and drunken fools acting out
their own drive-in movies.

Variations on the theme of
I WAS HERE. But someone else
was here too. And someone else.
Some dude even smashed
his car into the tennis practice wall
to test his own theory: why didn't it
collapse on top of him?

If the taped black horizon line
symbolizing net, rules, score-keeping,
morphed into a penis or snake or knife
or all three, if the words are illegible,
encoded or profane—and they are all that—
what fraction of sincerity
can get you a six-pack or even just a 40 oz.
at the party store across the street?

A practice wall for pissing
though no one needed practice.
It shaded raised and crumbled fault lines
of blacktop judged sufficient by men
who have not and never will
HIT THE BALL, STUPID!

Imaginary wall of future nightmare
smudged with factory dust,
graffiti scrawled as high as a hand

raised in a classroom by a boy
who never raised that hand.
This, this is his answer.

*

I am here and not here.
Build-it-and-they-will-come theory,
but no one came to hit a ball
only to have to hit it again.

We were raised on
the farther-you-hit-it theory
as explained to us in textbooks
we did not read or carry home.

So, if I did hit a tennis ball here once—
and I'm not saying I did—I hit it
over the damn wall and it rolled across
the parking lot toward the school's auto shop
which had its own perfectly good
windowless wall if someone so desired to—

desire. On a scale of one to ten
I smashed the mother-fucking scale
with a sledge hammer, given my aversion
to the subtlety of accuracy.

I, who tested another theory
at the tennis practice wall
one night with a girl I loved.
We stood unbuckled
and leaned into it
until it disappeared.

Up on Blocks

His father limping
from his stroke,
heaving his lunch pail
into the back of his pickup
like some stubborn, gimpy
shot putter, then driving off
to the job they gave him
after his rehab: steering
a hi-lo through the greasy plant

after Danny died

one day recovering on the porch
he hollered for the ice cream man
to stop, then bought us all popsicles

after Danny died

because his son—Vietnam—and so, and so.
He had a cough that could maul a lion
but he wouldn't stop smoking

after Danny died

Danny left his car, an absurdly red
Fury, up on blocks on our pocked street
to work on when he got home
but he never did, so

after Danny died

the car sat rusting—
no one touched it for years

till one night some asshole torched it
a whoosh heard down the block

and his father trembled and collapsed
in the terrible light of the flames

after Danny died

a tow truck dragged off the mess
gouging concrete into sparks as it pulled away

leaving charred cinderblocks like used-up Bibles,
and we dumped them in the weedy field
behind Bronco Lanes where they may be lying still

after Danny died

oh, the shame of the unmarked grave
somewhere off the end of our radio dials
while we fiddled with the blown fuses
of our cheap electric hearts

after Danny died

his father survived the second stroke
with one arm twitching. He returned to sit
on that porch, drooling odd noises,
flinging his good arm at flies. I sat with him
one afternoon for hours, then never again

after Danny died

because I was no saint and he was no prophet
and his pickup replaced the Fury
as the vehicle going nowhere
and his wife bagged groceries at the A&P

down the block and brought home
what she could carry

after Danny died

and we were fierce and serious boys
who would never go to war and thus
could always be fierce, and we too
smoked cigarettes and swore
and fucked and carried on like Danny did

before he died

and I have not mentioned his virgin bride
and the ramshackle wedding of a false
pregnancy annulled shortly after
but he had already signed up
that's the way it was on our street
of the hard luck and the harder

before and after Danny died

and he planted a bottle of Boone's Farm
on every table in the grade school cafeteria
and we squeezed onto tiny benches
and danced to Top 40 in front of the stage
where the bridal party sat

and he guzzled from the bottle
like the king of America
in his frilly tuxedo shirt,
and his father—Lord, his name
was Bruno—gave the saddest
toast I'd ever heard, then sat down
and smiled the beatific smile
of the damned and the oblivious

and I cannot remember it now
having drunk from the bottle myself
at fifteen. Nobody fought, and Bruno left happy,
and the bride and groom drove off in the Fury
toward the welcoming cliff and

after Danny died

the war ended quickly, and the ice cream man
got busted for selling drugs

we all stood at attention
at Bruno's funeral
like soldiers who had lost their general

because he had once bought us popsicles
because we would live forever

and no one burned the pickup
and his widow took to driving it
and one winter morning
I scraped her windows clear
then never again

after Danny died

because I had my own car, and it started
and ran, and I put on as many miles as I could

after Danny died.

LAZARUS IN THE SPRINKLER

Summer streets asizzle. Stranded
on the mirage of a square island
land-locked by Detroit grid.
Desert island. Ice cream man
circling in his pontoon party boat,
taunting us with the tainted music
of money. We drank Kool-Aid.
Sugar-red. Mouths sloppy with stain.

Our mothers sent us out under the sprinkler's
lone wing. We busted out in inspired,
interpretive dances—the story of an arc
of water more graceful than any human gesture
we knew. Holy water. Blessings.
God's liquid visitation and miracle,
evaporation on concrete, rainbow mist.
Quick tide of our slow, young lives approaching,
receding. We dared the sprinkler
to get us, dashing over or under—
as our father knew and could never forget,
always a matter of timing.

He pulled up front early in the black Ford:
a walkout at the plant—triple-digit heat.
He tossed his thermos and lunch box on the stoop
and lay down on our patch of brown grass
to let the water fall over him,
then back, then over him, like the hand
of God bringing him to life,
though we were the ones who lifted him up,
pulled him back from the dead.

Cutwoman in the Corner House

My mother the nurse, designated secret
sharer for women in flight angling across
the lined square grid of streets built by men.

Mrs. Anders tumbled, bruised, over the back fence,
Mrs. Blondell and the glass shard,
Mrs. Laney and the teeth, Mrs. Dodge and the burn—
my mother held ice against sobs.

If women in trouble emitted contrails,
the signals quickly dissipated, wind gusted,
dogs howled, husbands hammered and cursed,
red crosses scrawled in invisible ink, shades yanked down

against idling engines, twisted sirens, drunken hours.
My brothers and sisters pressed against the closed
kitchen door, our father at the factory, our TV ignited
for warmth—'60s situations without comedy.

The high-pitched alarm only women could hear
at our kitchen table between rounds—
what my mother did, forever dissipated. All we knew:
she patched them up, sent them home.

CHRISTMAS MIRACLE

Our father who art at home
and not at the factory
and not asleep
and not reclined
    and half-asleep
and not smoking and not drinking
    beer/coffee/or the symmetrical shots
with the firm thunder of their landing
at the yellow kitchen table
angry at life's ponzi scheme,
rigged deck, ship anchored in sand.

In the basement, he saws and pounds
scraps of wood from half-done home repairs,
slaps on primer and hauls it upstairs
held up like an offering to the almighty tax collector

and that night we have a candle-lit procession
from the bathroom to the living room
my sister cupping Jesus in her tiny hands—
    are we singing a hymn?
    Are the tree lights sparking?
Our candles in tin foil to catch the wax
    my brothers and I surround
my father's newly built stable
    as she eases Jesus
into his cotton-padded manger.
    Are we angels in our ragged robes?
    Is there a cardboard star?

My father in his chair
    not cursing the wise men.

First Communion

My parents' gift: a missal.
In the photo, I hold it, wedged between
them in front of St. Anne's in my brush cut
and maroon sport coat. A holy card
from Sister Maureen marks my place:
I hope you stay as close to Jesus
as you are today.

I cut out the heart to hide my stash:
a lid, papers, roach clip, pipe,
a chunk of hash. Lots of prayers,
I noticed, cutting them out, praying
not to get busted. I hid the book
under my dented Electric Football.

*

Where's my book? My book? I asked my brother,
tearing apart the closet, plastic linemen scattering.

A week later, my father cornered me,
my mother out shopping: *I found something*
of yours, he said. *Look at me when I'm talking*
to you.
        I stared off, swirling into black-
light posters: *Why were you going through*
my stuff? I had a new stash in my pocket.
He couldn't punish me without telling her.

*

I sold it out of the basement,
new friends stopping by
for brief exchanges. Pounds
stuffed in a beanbag chair.

I kept that prayer book hollow
and stayed as close to high as I could
for long, tunneling years.
I should have looked him in the eye,
met him in the air between us.

What words did I cut out and toss?
My father threw out the pot,
but we could not throw out
what we did not have, could not save
what we could not see or find
while I looked away from him
in that tiny room
with the door closed.

CRACK THE WHIP

Endless downpour had splattered
the campground into gray mud.
We bought rawhide whips
at the pseudo-Indian tourist
shop in Muskegon. Our bleary father
paid, wanting only to be beery,
his vacation washing away. Leaky
tent, wet matches, droopy cigarettes.

Perhaps that explains my brother
crafting a lethal tomahawk
for my son on a rainy vacation
35 years later. My wife flung it
in the lake where it sunk
with a plunk as my brother
and son both cried out.

In the basement back home,
we cracked those whips to hear
whose echoed loudest. We strutted
city sidewalks, flicking wildly at trees,
bushes, cats, dogs, and younger children.
It hurt. We knew it hurt.

The store offered no Indian explanation
for the whips, nor the display case
of switchblades and stilettos
imported from Mexico, illegal except
in that square mile of local politics.

The whips hung on hooks
near our mother scrubbing laundry

under a crucifix dangling above washtubs.
The old saints whipped themselves
for God. Jesus, sweet Jesus.

The cheap dyed feathers of my headdress
fell out in the car when my father reached back
to smack somebody. At home, our streets ran
long and straight. Our whips curled
into frayed snakes, live wires sparking.

Nothing is simple. I apologize for suggesting
otherwise. Eyes watered with pain.
Apologies never enough. Whip—
—lash! Gnashing sound bitten off.

Those whips could still be landing
on somebody. My mother prayed
to merciful Jesus while my father swore
in the name of God the Father, the cruel one.

The cracked whip of our laughter
at the howls of pain. You can only
crack a whip at the air so many times.
Trust me. Or, better yet, don't.
Throw the tomahawk in the lake.

II.

The Wave, Tiger Stadium

My brother and I took our grandfather to a game—
     1984—we'd win it all that year, a tough team
a man who'd watched Cobb could appreciate. Six months
     after his heart attack, he wobbled down the ramp
between us to our left field seats. Thin and ashy as a cigarette,
     though he never smoked. If you called him a simple man,
he would not disagree, a mechanic at Packard's who lost
     two kids when they were still kids, lost his job
when he still needed work, lost his wife over and over,
     though still she sat strapped to a chair
          in a sour antiseptic room.

     The Wave was new, and Detroit embraced
its odd magic, how you could both stay in one place
     and move, to counter the ritualized
machinery of the game. The tang of anarchy
     sweet to anyone who worked an assembly line
and knew about standing in place,
     as we all had done. We pulled him
to his feet each time the wave passed, watched him
     swing his hands up and smile his random crooked
teeth. We never saw him raise his hands, before or after.
     Before mascots and Jumbotrons and piped-in rock,
orchestrated fan instructions. The Wave. He died at 96
     without drama or complaint. He never stood out—
shied from both tears and hearty laughter.
     We never heard about our dead aunt and uncle—
not from him, not ever. But once he stood and raised
     his hands to the sky among 50,000 others.
He shouted our names when he saw it circling
     so we'd be quick to lift him. Now, I call it testifying
or joy. I'm not sure what our father would've called it,

he who worked nights tying brake cables,
who paid his father's bills, weighed down by the unspoken,
he who knew their names, and ours.
He who could not wave back.

GRANDFATHER RENTS TO PIMP

We were escaping him from Detroit
to a smaller, crappier house in Warren
next to his sister Martha and her maiden
daughter Irene with the mangled hand
who worked for Quaker Oats, highlighting
her life with free boxes of Cap'n Crunch.
We borrowed Mr. Carson's van before he
himself escaped to Arizona, a retired postal
worker tired of dodging wild dogs
and delivering mail to burned-out
abandoned or simply empty lots
of the city, the absurd anti-logic
of it, bags full of mail to Santa Claus
on the Moon, no forwarding address,
not even junk mail to mark their territory
like the dogs casually chewing
the bones of other postmen.
We humored Grandpa on the house—
no one paid cash money
for swampland in the hood, crackheads
the only interested observers, and even then
it was a buyer's market. But he found
Reverend Saint Pierre who wanted
to rent rooms to hookers he was rehabbing,
taking them off the street. Grandpa
wouldn't know a hooker if one bit him
on the ass like one of those wild dogs,
much less that he'd have to pay extra for that.

Rev gives Grandpa a month's rent
and Grandpa thinks he's going to be
shitting gold bricks the rest of his life—

but you know from the title that
Rev. St. Pierre's preaching a different
gospel, and when Grandpa keeps going
back to pick up things we'd deliberately
abandoned, particularly his collection
of plastic milk cartons, he notices
the Rev don't got no collar,
no vestments, not even a damn cross
on the thick gold chain round his neck,
and then, of course, there ain't no second
month's rent, and my father's not paying
water or electric anyway, writing letters
to the city conceding everything—
take my house, please—and Grandpa
loses his license for driving too slow
on those streets where nobody
should be stopping unless they got
an appointment with the Rev
or a standing order at crack house #3,
so Grandpa watches TV in the tinier house
that boots Grandma out into madness
at the earliest opportunity—suddenly
she can't find the bathroom
because the only bathroom
she's ever known is full of hookers
crosstown—and tells us the Rev's ladies
wore jock straps and he didn't know
what sport they played. Oh, Grandpa,
what are we gonna do with you?

We waved the white flag
on our way out of town while
I spilled scalding coffee on my lap
to stay alive behind the wheel of that van
spewing black exhaust. Mr. C gave me all
his thick socks and insulated postal gloves

because he was going someplace
warm and dry where they'd imported
the London Bridge, though they had
no water in Arizona except the drinking
fountain at the Sunoco station. Back
in Detroit, Grandpa spends that one
month's rent on a new drill
and a lifetime supply of racial epithets,
the arteries of his beloved city hardening
and, damn it, ya gotta blame somebody,
and the Reverend didn't last a year
without utilities, though the crackheads
might still be there—like roaches,
they can survive nuclear shenanigans—
and being a white guy born in that city
I have only the cynical patter
of the sideline reporter,
but when I think of hookers turning
tricks in those rooms, those beds
of my childhood, I regret
leaving behind grandma's music box,
the tiny dancer alone
waiting for the fire.

Ankle Beach, Lake Huron

We stumbled over stones at Ankle Beach—
so named by my oldest brother. Our grandfather only
let us wade—he could not swim and save us.

We couldn't see across the cold blue to Canada
or even imagine it. Why tease us with all
that water, stuck on the shore at Ankle Beach?

He never told us about his son/our uncle who died at fifteen
when his appendix burst. Years later, a stranger did.
All we knew was grandpa would not swim and save us.

He thrilled at freighters in the distance, wondering what
they carried, where they were destined while he stood anchored.
My father kept the secret, his face a flat stone at Ankle Beach.

Grandpa's shack sat safely back, a half mile from the beach.
Silver insulation between studs reflected where his hammer
stopped. He could not swim nor save. Us?

Lying in bed, we heard night waves crash against shore.
Icy water numbed us with God's silence. He watched
us heave rocks into the lake at Ankle Beach,
the heavier the better. He could not swim. Save us.

FLIGHTLESS

My mother got mugged in the driveway
after second shift at rehab. Keyless,
she pounded the door in the aftermath.
Manufactured hysteria of Detroit TV news
and the last of a six-pack drowned her out
till the old man woke to my mother mugged.
The drive-way, cracked, muted cement under dim
porch light. Blood clotted her hair, stained her white
uniform. Dazed drunk, he opened the door.
In the aftermath, neighbors moved out. The race
was on. Race was on. For us: brighter lights?
More prayers? He raised the volume to deafen
my mother. Mugged-in-the-driveway
her new middle name on our white street.
The men were black, I should've said sooner.
Fearless, she pounded on doors in the aftermath
to beg neighbors to meet, not move. My father got
a gun, I should've said sooner. Silence had its way with me.
My mother did not mug for cameras or drive away
but the doors were closed and locked ever after.

THE MACULAR DEGENERATION BOOGIE

a story from the Lives of the Saints, Blind Edition

My mother, bad magician,
mad scientist, limping dancer,
blind juggler in the kitchen,
dips her fingers into measuring cups,
traces the S and P on shakers,
waits for dough to rise in the broiler,
dials spinning counter-blind-wise,
the oven still stinking with burn-off
from last week's erupting lasagna
and hot cross buns turned to holy rocks
to stone St Lucy, the patron saint
of blindness.

St Lucy carries her eyes on a plate
in paintings like a server of hors d'oeuvres
at a reception. My blind mother
might ask, *what are these?* or maybe
just pop one in her mouth and be surprised.

She now finds surprise
to be overrated, she who always
loved the mad tingle of the un-
expected, her open-mouthed
laughter spreading like heat
from an open oven.

It's as if she carved all her recipes
into a bar of soap, then washed her hands.
She limps back and forth to the cruel buzzing
of the giant Martian timer.

Stubborn as any martyr
she has faith in both God
and not dying, not curling
into herself like a poisoned worm
in her special chair cushioned
against her back's steel rods.

She cooks. Is cooking.
Continues to cook. My father lurks
with the fire extinguisher.
She cuts him a piece of cake
in the shape of the state of
Oklahoma? West Virginia?
He shuts up and eats.
He tells her it is good.
She made him sick last week.

When he tries to help, the air burns
like melting plastic on a careless burner.
I remember the pattern of her pinched crusts,
perfect waves lapping against the edges.
Now it's *man the lifeboats.*
She's bent over, knife just inches
from her nose. Her hip's shot.
Her life crooked. Her rosary lost.

She tried to get the dough to rise
in winter sun streaming in,
but even sun's turned against her,
despite her special orange glasses
and wide-brimmed hat, a desperado
waiting for her cue, but no one's
giving her a clue. The timer erupts again
or the smoke alarm or the telephone
with its mysterious disappearing numbers.

I'm sure you have a lot of advice for us.
Leave a phone message.
They never check the machine.
My father's going to get a red flag
to tie to her walker so when summer
comes she can limp across the street
to the store where they know her well enough
to take her list and walk her down the aisles.

She listens to a book on tape. Her eyes
on a plate. Dinner ready soon.
Hungry yet?

Grilled Cheese at the Rehab Center

A menu option at every meal,
       and my mother takes it—
perfect food for the blind
       easily gripped
no excess spilled onto the plate
       or smeared across her face.
Cheese, the glue holding it all together.
       Like the gripped hands of prayer.
And it's warm with the greasy illusion
       of a cooked meal.
              Fuck the pasta,
the peas, the uncut meat, and in God's Holy Name,
       fuck the soup.
Oh, the dignity of the grilled cheese
       almost dainty in her clawed fingers.

KEY TO THE COTTAGE

My father gave me a key
to his retirement cottage in Newaygo
on a tributary of the Muskegon.
Cottage—a family euphemism
for the small gray trailer with a room
built on, three hours from Detroit
and the scabbed streets we grew up on.

33 years at Ford's. He cuts down trees
and burns them in bonfires. High flames
to throw a little fear in his veins
or burn out the sludge from the dark
cavities of those numb years.

The notion that a key is needed—
a family myth, symbolism for the eyes
of the beholders. You could break in
with a blade of grass. Newaygo, Newaygo,
he chants like a native, salmon fighting
upstream each fall under his tainted eye.

No one can blame him if he shoots
one with his bow and arrow or pins one
to the silty bottom with his pitchfork.
If he wrestles one from the shallows
and beats it to death.

HOUSE OF DRUMMING, HOUSE OF SONG

Here in Pittsburgh, my teenage son and daughter
sing their carefree, fizzy joy. Digging
in the yard, I hear their voices
rise and fall through open windows.
They can carry a tune. They have pockets
big enough, sewn by minor gods
with magic thread and endless dreaming.

In Detroit, we never sang.
Not the boys, not the girls.
We listened to rock so loud our ears
smoked, but we were not singers.
We drummed car seats, dashboards,
and each other. We lit lighters
and held them aloft at arena shows.

How could singing be for sissies
when our heroes sang? Equations
and formulas, mysteries and historical texts,
electrical currents and gym class ordeals,
red arrows and one-way streets, woofers
and tweeters and teeters and totters
all led to the same factory boats,
both anchored and beached on the shore
of the Lake of Industry where we would row
in sand to the gritty stop of retirement,
bailing water the whole time, mechanizing even
our dreams, cutting them short with precision tools
so that breathing itself became our only song.

We lost the hook. Never found the refrain.
We played extended drum solos identical

to our fathers' while the crowd slipped away
to the john, or felt each other up, or passed joints,
or simply nodded off, while the rest of the band
drifted into shadows of dazed drinking.
When they returned, we accepted polite applause
for our endurance and steadfast lack of creativity.

My father never sang. In the middle of dust mopping,
my mother sometimes swept into song, grabbing
the closest child and howling—Ozzy Osbourne
channeling Patsy Cline at warp speed.
She seemed so happily out of herself
that we fled. Laughing, she chased us.
We laughed too, afraid of wanting
to be caught.

I still don't sing except alone
in fast-moving automobiles, though I left
that old life long ago, the heavy-metal job,
the muffled solitary drumming,
long lines of tiny bodies, somebody smirking
that we all look alike from above.

I dropped through the trap door
and into what I've been calling my life
for the last thirty years. If there's a beat
of a different drum, I have not heard it.

I want to carry one long note
that slowly sinks into silence.
My family jokes that our "Happy Birthday"
gets dogs a-howling, so we avoid even that—
straight to cake and ice cream.
We vote for listening, we vote
for mad clapping. We vote for golden
oldies. We endorse the air guitar
and the broomstick mike of lip-synching.

My mother hobbled by daily pain—
I have not heard her sing
in two thousand years. Math
and song, entirely outside
the singed circle of our existence.

My mother, a red planet
on her own rectangular urban orbit.
I want to hear her say, *you don't like
my singing? I'll just sing louder
and longer.* A lesson we should've
learned: to hell with polite applause.

Even the weeds enjoy getting pulled,
or so I imagine, freed by the dazzle and flash
and sheer volume of my children's young voices,
the sound waves on their way to Mars or Cincinnati
or to the mobile home in Sterling Heights, Michigan

where my 85-year-old parents are just now stirring,
and perhaps while my father makes coffee
and my blind mother attempts to butter toast,
not her fingers, somebody, against
all odds, might briefly
and quietly
hum.

III.

Short Guide to the Addiction Memoir

ADDICTION MEMOIR, SHORT VERSION

I'm here to tell you.

ADDICTION MEMOIR, SHORTER VERSION

I'm back.

ADDICTION MEMOIR, SHORTEST VERSION

Sorry.

ADDICTION MEMOIR, ALTERNATE VERSION

Hey, look at me, up on the Jumbotron!

ADDICTION MEMOIR, OMNISCIENT VERSION

He had too much to drink and was being an asshole again.

POSTSCRIPT

He's sober, and he's still an asshole.

ADDICTION MEMOIR SELF-ACTUALIZED EPIPHANY AND CAR WASH

If I could've stopped while I was ahead, I wouldn't be here in the first place.

ADDICTION MEMOIR ONE-UPMANSHIP

I slept with my sister *and* my father, then OD'd on goat's milk vodka extract while climbing Mt. Everest with my monkey lover.

ADDICTION MEMOIR, FAUX DISCLAIMER

My penis is, in fact, very large.

ADDICTION MEMOIR, THESIS STATEMENT

The truth will either set you free or bore you to death.

ADDICTION MEMOIR, STARTLING CONFESSION

I was so stoned I can't remember.

FOOTNOTES:

Coals to Newcastle.

Hair of the Yippy Dog.

Preaching Naked to the Choir.

ADDICTION MEMOIR, SEQUEL

Hey, I'm back on the Jumbotron!

THE ADDICT'S GUIDE TO FATHERHOOD

I placed a soft red rug at the bottom of the stairs to catch
my children when they fell. I clipped the commas
of their fingernails like an obsessed grammarian.
I collected the pebbles *they'd* collected and discarded.
I discarded my own collections—empty bottles, needles.
I vacuumed up the dusty street I'd rode in on.
I clapped the erasers together, white dust offered up
to the god of pure intentions. Sun block and ipecac syrup.
Dream weavers and wind catchers. A kindly dentist
with a bubble machine and fairy assistants.
An old-school pediatrician with his home phone number.
Elmo Band-Aids and Scooby Doo Underoos and Beatrix Potter
everything else. Baby gates and universal childproofing.
Glow-in-the-dark stars glued on
so the sky would not fall on them.

HAIR ON FIRE

We ironed fall leaves
        between wax-paper sheets.
We melted crayons into candles
        and froze Kool-Aid into popsicles.
We poked cloves into oranges. We grew roots
        on sweet potatoes tooth-picked in water.
We taped our broken glasses together
        and shut up. We made shoe-box
dioramas with Play-Doh and modeling clay.
        We cut snowflakes from folded paper
and hung them with kite string.
        We made newspaper kites
and imagined they could fly.

We shaped tin foil into fake coins
        for our church envelopes.
We covered love bites with Kool-Aid.
        We filled liquor bottles with holy water.
We hid our stash in beanbag chairs.
        We drove to Ohio for drugs
and rolled back our father's odometer.
        We mounted our girlfriends
on basement pool tables, clacking balls together
        for ears upstairs.
We drew lies with chalk
        and the truth with tar.
We lit our hair on fire
        to cover the smell.

STAGGER

Strung-out girl in a pink mini-
skirt staggers through the club's gravel
parking lot looking for someone
with the band. She drops
her sparkly silver bag. She wants
to know do I have any blow.
She kisses me hard. I kiss back.
Let's fuck in the gravel, she says.
I cough a laugh.
Between these cars.

Her eyes, melted diamonds.
Let's not talk about *my* eyes—
the camera doesn't lie
when it's turned off. Her microdot
skirt, long white legs spread
in blue parking-lot light.

I did not get down on my knees
and fuck her like a dog.
Time shut its steel door
while we staggered there.
I didn't want. I wanted.
She was an inflatable groupie doll
for—what band was it? ELO?
HELLO? She wobbled into me.
You're with the band, right?

I wish I could say I did the right
thing, and for good reasons.
But I'd spun on that planet before,
searching for signs of life. I wanted her

to be more *there* at least. More *with*.
Thin, pale—long brown hair swaying
in tilted light like fuses, like the tarnished
shimmering curtains of a striptease.
The band? How would that make her
happier? I was stoned lonely myself,
and a few beers in. Smeared ink
of the bottom line. We never saw stars
above Detroit, so why even look up?

I waved in the universal symbol for surrender
or refusal. She wore a tiny gold cross.
Your loss, I think she said. She screwed
a heel into gravel. *How about a smoke then?*
and raised two fingers to her mouth.
I abandoned her to artificial night. She leaned
against one of the cars we were to fuck between.
No filter for memory's cigarette. Did she
find someone with the band? She wasn't old
enough to get inside.

I curled my hands to hide factory grease
while out of nowhere thick grief wormed
into my chest. Music shoved its way through
cinder block, rose and fell from the club's
distant door. Fuck me in the gravel.
I was with the band once, I said.
Not anymore.

Last Day in Coldwater

Our phone died due to lack
of payment. I left her a note
and trudged down gray splintered steps.

She was tangled tight in her weekly
sleep of the dead, the morning crash
after the stairs burned down beneath her
after days of artificially sustained
floating above scorched earth.

Paying bills required
a certain sustained attention.
We had cold water
and nothing more.

Unwritten debts were due.
They had the steepest
interest.

Listening to the blue music
of our veins, we had broken
unwritten rules and red-tagged
our whereabouts.

I walked through dawn and into
hunger, past the sizzle-stench
of burnt coffee and the shrinking
menu of our young lives.

We were close to Ohio,
closer to Indiana. Michigan
did not want us. We had no friends.
They had exploded

in one of our many miracles gone
wrong. She slept with hands limp
over the foldout couch—our bed.

She'd want a fix when she awoke
to wind her clock. How many pencils
can you accumulate, erasers eroded
by lies, before you toss them all?

Disconnected. Perhaps the recorded
message might briefly fool those out
to find us. Precision lost

its wings, then the wheels fell off.
In lieu of fiscal responsibility,
we repossessed each other. The wind
swung wide across the flat land. My face

stung with radioactive love. For her,
for it, and what came first? The drugs.
The drugs came first, so I mention them
last. Someone was going to climb the stairs

and it wouldn't be me, and what
would they demand? I should've
woken her, but I did not. I should've
shaken the map in her face.

Look where we are,
I should have said.

CHANGING THE NAME

While his wife was at church
my great-grandfather let his son choke
on a chicken bone while he mopped out
his tavern's Saturday night stink

then drank himself out of the bar, dying
in a freight elevator filled with Uniroyal's rubber
stench. When I missed my plane in Grand Rapids,
too stoned to read the watch face, I had to stay

an extra night, lighting and blowing out
imaginary candles while my two babies
back home kept my wife up talking in tongues
about their stoned old man.

Great-grandfather Julius Danneels
got divorced, changed the name to Daniels,
gave away his pet monkey,
but nothing erased the boy turning blue.

I inherited the watch Julius won racing pigeons,
a fancy piece too complicated to fix,
yet I hear it ticking.

Witnesses

I was painting the hall and stairway
"River Mist" when Witnesses knocked at the door

looking so sincere I wanted to pelt them
with water balloons. The dog next door

already barking. *I don't have cable*, I said.
That's why we're here, they said.

I raised my River Mist hands over my face
in a protective stance familiar to monster movie

aficionados. It never saves anyone, and they
weren't going to save me. I was drowning

in that misty river. Next door, my neighbor
was photographing his own crumbling house—

for posterity? *Go away!* I shouted. Someone wanted
to steal a small portion of my soul. *I need that soul!*

The cable guy was tougher: *everyone on your street
has cable*, he said. *What's wrong with you?*

I don't believe! I cried. *In cable!* They all left pamphlets
in my mail slot claiming my damnation.

One channel versus 99. River Mist vs.
The Man in the Moon. The selling of souls

at an introductory rate. No one else ever
knocks on my door. Where have all the other

salesmen gone? Perhaps my neighbor has them locked
in his basement. They skip his house completely—

monster weeds, peeling paint, collapsing porch—
disconnected satellite dish picking up unholy signals.

River Mist. Blood on my hands. River missed. God's will.
If I had cable, I'd get the Monster Movie Channel.

It's the paint. It's the ladder. It's the total coverage.
Why are they really here? What constitutes

a sale? A good day? Who cooks the books
for Jesus? How does anyone dress for success?

I wear my holey jeans. Paint blurs my knees.
If I knelt to pray, there'd be evidence.

THE LINCOLN DEATH CHAIR

...a dark stain on the red upholstery of the back of the chair due to soiling from the hair pomade that was fashionable for men at the time. This was once thought to be the president's blood, but it is not.

A field trip to Greenfield Village,
Henry Ford's outdoor museum. Henry, one
of Detroit's gods, but we were in 9ᵗʰ grade
and he was just somebody our fathers worked for,
even if he was dead.

Andy and Pete and I dumped out half a bottle
of Coke, refilled it with rum in the weeds
behind Bronco Lanes next to school,
a furtive *fuck you* to the yellow bus
idling by the auto shop.

Henry/Hank Ford, fuck you too. We weren't
going to disappear inside your factories
like our fathers. I stashed the bottle
in my lunch bag. Why get drunk
to visit the Wright brothers' workshop,
Edison's lab, the bored blacksmith
sweating by his fire?

Why not? Warm by the time we passed it
around between bites of bologna sandwiches.
We fell asleep on the bus home,
but I'm getting ahead of myself.

Getting ahead of ourselves perhaps
was the point, though to try to get a point,
we could sharpen our pencils down to stubs
and still have nothing.

The next year Andy's dad died
in a car crash. Andy in the backseat,
his cool sunglasses exploding.
Pete became Peter and started getting
too friendly in a way that didn't cut it
at our school.

My son's in 9th grade. The idea of him drinking
sprays buckshot into my chest. I don't know
what he's doing in his room with the door
closed. Well, I kind of know.

If he could take a field trip
to where I've been, would he want
the bus to pull over and let him
puke his guts out?

Pete, hunched over roadside gravel,
retched while we watched.
Mrs. Kerman told the driver
it was that bug going around.

I killed that bug twice in my life,
and I swear I'll never have to kill it again.
Ever since I got stoned and missed
a flight home to my children.

We stood in front of the chair Lincoln
was shot in—all we wanted to see
in the whole damn museum: the stain.

I threw away my apple. The cute girls wanted
nothing to do with us, enamored
with Orville and Wilbur in Ye Olde Cycle Shop.

We were looking for our parts,
trying to figure out how they fit together.
My son's doing that upstairs
with his headphones on and his computer
tuned to a string of xxxxxs.

No one's disappeared from his life yet,
seeping away into the big wide world,
the gluttonous slob of a world, the whale's mouth,
the tunnel on the turnpike, the disconnected phones.

I followed our trails long enough to know
that we all did, at least for a time, work
for Mr. Henry Ford. Rum and Coke
for breakfast. Coke and Rum for lunch.

The glassblower, the candle maker, the wool spinner,
didn't stand a chance in Henry's world.
I suppose that wasn't the lesson for the day.

I wrote my paper about Lincoln's roped-off
chair. I waited for the crowd
to thin, hoping to sneak a feel, but it never did.

Abraham/Abe, dude, man, tough luck, buddy.
I clenched the golden rope. I wrote about—
I don't remember what, but got marked
down for claiming it was blood

when it was proven to be pomade,
greasy heads leaning back
in the darkness of Ford Theater, waiting
for the show to begin.

Dusk, July, Third Floor

Up here, parallel with the skyline,
I watch dark change to darker. 8:21 pm EST.
My old friend Chris disappeared into EST.

Showed up one day divorced, wanting to talk
about how we *really felt* about everything.
A quarter pound of pot stashed under my pillow

like a semi-permanent gift from the tooth fairy,
but he was intent on not doing one up,
talking about how good it felt to scream and tell

the truth. He unloaded eight years of resentment
on me when I only deserved about four. I still
did not tell him I once slept with his ex-wife

while he lay snoring in the next room.
In my attic, I'm sweating remembered pleasure,
ears burning with the harsh buzz of betrayal,

but it's worth it to see that line fade above the hillside
until all is black, and the past does not matter,
and maybe some couple's on that hill getting

their butts grass-stained and groaning softly
and seeing my tiny lit window
and calling it a star.

IV.

Ohio Turnpike Opens New Rest Stop

A smashed bee quivers on my windshield.
My daughter sings "The Sound of Music"
though there are no hills, nothing alive.

In her car seat behind me, she wants
that bee gone. The wipers smear it
stubborn across the glass.

We talk about Nazis and nuns. We both
have to go, but wait for the new stop
with the private family bathroom

though when we finally arrive
we stand squirming for minutes
until a woman unlocks the door

and steps out alone, eyes glazed
with locked-door drugs, the sting
of recognition.

My daughter did not want to get out
of the car. I said *no Nazis here,*
no bees here—more lies.

I brushed the dead one away.
I held her hand. I led her in.

Premature Aging

A sideways storm that brought down
my favorite tree blew water

through the screens and across
the ancient blue-black linoleum

where it pinned my white papers
to each other and to the attic floor.

They dry yellow and crisp. I try
to pry edges apart, to recall

what I had to say. Across the street
in the park, sympathy notes and flowers

gather where the tree's leafy umbrella
gave us all lower-case hope in the cool

wispy shade of 150 years. My daughter
weeps on the stump. We'll all be dead

before another tree could rise
that high, that wide, its own green sky.

The ink spread, sank through the layers,
loosening its grip.

The clouds are boats, and those squealing
brakes on the street below, maybe

they're just sweet little dolphins
destroying my memory.

Look on the bright side. The shiny side.
The smiley-face side. The rainbow side.

I have my buckets in place. My son
took the biggest fossil from the Carnegie's

Nature Camp and plunked it on my desk
for Father's Day along with a number

of smaller rocks. And a list of what they all were
on a sheet of paper I am trying to pry loose.

The clock clicks 3:37. I can spend all day here
and apparently nearly have. I am in love

with the big fossil, some shelled creature,
35 segments curled around its center.

It will hold down any stack of papers. Rain
bounces off. What about scissors? If you riff

too far on the truth, you end up cutting the string.
How can anyone concentrate with a wood chipper

and chain saws and the ice cream man's
mechanical yodel? If I could separate these two sheets,

I might have an answer for you. If I could get my daughter
to stop crying over a tree. If I could just cry myself.

Slow Learner

A nearby town claims
never to have fog. What do they do
with such clarity? Wouldn't it hurt?

I spent twenty years of my life
creating artificial fog. Before that,
I spent ten years trying to create

the S sound.
I watch my odometer turn.
Why did I drink so much?

Once I felt invincible. Even
with my stomach torn apart
my only goal was to drink again.

Why does my knee ache this morning?
The S of escape. At age forty
I finally learned how to whistle

blowing love into my daughter's hair.

IF YOU EVER HAVE TO DO THIS YOURSELF

My daughter started crying
when she couldn't get the fake poop back
into the fake butt of the Pooping Dog
she won at the school carnival. She'd squeezed
too hard, and popped the poop out
in the car on the way home. We'd eaten
half-frozen fries and gristly hot dogs.
All for a good cause.

She's in first grade. My son's in third.
His dog still has its poop. She doesn't want me
to say *potty* anymore—too babyish—
yet she was bawling. I lost it, screaming
to scare us all. Back home, I got them
into bed, my daughter still snuffling, my son
glazed over into silence.

Shamed, I stood in the kitchen jamming
the orange rubber cylinder of poop
back up the plastic dog's butt.
I used index finger, I used thumb,
I used tack hammer. I wet the poop,
then squeezed with needle-nose pliers

until I got it all back in.
Two Pooping Dogs on the counter
for them to find in the morning.
To write their names on in Sharpie.

They kissed me when I awoke.
They held their puppies. We have no pets,
though they're always asking.

If you ever have to do this yourself,
keep it together. Shut up
and do love's dirty work.

THE NAMES OF DINOSAURS

I spent an endless era with my children
visiting bones at the Carnegie—from stroller
to toddlers to sliders on slick tiled floor.
We've got the best dino bones. Others make casts
of *our* bones to fake people out.
                                    Why do kids
love dinosaurs? (Most kids, most dinosaurs.)
Daddy's home! Daddy's home! They'd rush a-tumble
when I got home from work. What made me
think of that is—
                        did I say they're teenagers now?—
today I found a plastic dino under the basement stairs
I could not name. Well, *Bob*—what we called all dinosaurs.
 I once knew the names
                            of all the damn sauruses.
Daddy-o's long gone. The kids grunt like cave dwellers
at every eager inquiry into their lives. Teenagers
never go extinct. No tar pits for them. What giant boulder
rocked our world into this?
                              With prodding,
my daughter tells me it's a *triceratops*,
then tosses it in the trash. I want to press
my luck, ask her, does she remember those weekdays
at the museum, no crowds. Just us!
Dust motes floating through high windows.
Jell-O in the cafeteria with workers at lunch smiling
at your cuteness?
                    Oh, the big, high bones above us,
xylophone tails, grisly teeth, thick slabs. The incredible
stillness, so quiet that…I could hear the love
beating in their eager hearts?

Nah. A modern stone-age family,
we lug around our stones of silence—

no wonder
I can't remember the names. I used to steal my father's beers
from a red and yellow case under the stairs. Stroh's 16 oz.
returnable bottles (33 percent more). Warm beer. I burped,
made faces, and guzzled.

Teenagers. Another long boring story
told by a mean, tired dad. Did dinosaurs make noises?
In the movies they always do. *Raaaaahr!* I wouldn't want
to be around when a dinosaur had to go—

know what I mean?
Throw in a P word and get the kids to laugh. *Poop!*
Today my son says he hates me. *Double poop!* Climate change,
it'll kill you every time.

Right, Steggy? Right, Dippy?
T-Rex thunders down the stairs, fresh from a growth spurt.
We're all meat eaters here.

Hey, remember, the museum's
just down the street—the sun shone through, so peaceful
even extinction took on a rosy hue! As long as I could be with you.
Yeah, you,

I'm talking to you.
Look at me when I'm talking to you.

THE CAUCUS OF MY GREAT FALL

I changed my clocks
as I was told.
They said it was
for my own good.
My own food?
I asked, deaf
to clichés
while living my own.

We took a vote,
they said. *What*
about mine? I asked.
I twirled the flaming baton
of the minute hand.
When they said
you can stop now

I said *say when*
but then cranked up
the volume of my mad
cranked-up life.
I fell back, I sprung for-
ward. I fell forward.
They said I was hurting
myself. And I said *ouch ouch,*

a dog barking in the obscure language
of the heart—I mean, of damage.
My needle was my metronome
and my pitch was my catch.
I slurred my words in time
with the world's blur.

Adjust the speed, they said.
To make us love you again, they said.

They, the faces in the room.
There's a name for this gathering
but that too is a cliché, so I have
forgotten it. A surprise party
for addicts. No balloons,
no cake. *You can stop now,*
they said. *No, I can't,*
I said. *Once upon a time,* I said.

Together, we watched
clock hands strangle each other
in the post-game fireworks display.
That's not what we meant, they said.
I knew what they meant. I wasn't
hungry. For my finale, I threw
the red-hot baton in the air.
I punched out the clock's face.

I waited for the standing O
to leave the stadium
of my own crowded kitchen,
but they were so happy
clarifying my demise, recapping
the big game of my life,
the big choke, I decided
to lay low. I did math

problems in my head.
I went digital on them. I caved
in on myself. I yelled
timber and *fore*
and I folded my hands
into the church

of all the people
being gone

but that prayer
didn't have a rosary
of a chance. They held
up cards to rate
my performance.
They were all blank.
For my next trick,
I said, and somebody,

despite promising not to,
walked out. *Elvis has
left the building*,
I said, and some-
body said *shut up*,
just please, shut up.
Finally, I opened
the faint praise of my gifts.

I dutifully thanked them all,
and they took me away.
And if you think
that's a happy ending,
I will show you my drawer
full of bent arrows.

Posted Limits

Startled by night weeds
        and a lost semi moaning
up the hill on the boulevard into the park
        as I walk for milk at the mini-mart

escaping weather reports and talk radio
        falling into desire for reckless destination
and nostalgia for the glow-speck
        of cigarette and dream remnant

before I started taking those dream-
        erasing pills. Maybe the truck
is not lost, simply breaking the law
        late-night running on forbidden streets.

Just milk, and the twang of regret watching
        the straggle-stumble of closing time
at Uncle Jimmy's. I strangle sobriety
        into a withered candle.

I cup my hands around
        the imaginary match
            and blow.

Spinning Donuts in Universal City Parking Lot

Laid off again. Pick a year, any year.
Pick a recession, any recession. Down-
turn. Slump, chump.

We used to eat big plastic bags
of puffed wheat for breakfast
when my father was home,

laid off. Once, he poured too much milk
and all the floating puffs
erupted onto the kitchen table,

then the floor. He laughed his ass off,
so we all laughed too, milk streaming out
our noses. We rolled on the floor

because our father knew everything.
I'd pay a million bucks to hear him
laugh like that again. High-pitched,

out of nowhere, a little crazy.
But a million dollars won't do it,
seeing as it'd take bringing the old man

back from the grave. I'm sober
if the cops stop me. Kids of my own
who haven't heard me laugh like that

since—since… The whole damn mall's
abandoned. Ghost mall. They hold meetings
to discuss its future. They've boarded up

what they can, but kids with rocks,
they'll find glass to smash. If my house
were bigger, I'd have more to do to fill

these days. They hold meetings to discuss
its future—Chrysler, Ford, GM. Take your pick.
Downsizing the upturn. Renegotiating the reneges.

Go for a ride, my wife says. *Burn off
some steam.* Renegotiate some steam. Snow
relentless. I can't blame snow, can I?

In high school, I got caught shoplifting a belt
at Federal's department store. My father
appreciated the irony as he whipped me with his.

I'm saying, I miss my father times like this
when the clock is stuck, and hammering
doesn't help, just mangles the hands

like a punch press. He had these deep
eyes like he'd seen all the ghosts and nothing
scared him. I spin the wheel, and the car whirls

into circles. I would've brought the kids along
if that didn't seem so damn crazy. I'm half-
surprised there's no one else out here tonight.

Even the floodlights dark.
Nobody can see me spinning.
Nobody can see me laugh.

FLIGHT

I'm looking for the last cloud's
dark lining, the last true sin
for those who didn't stop counting.
Why demand bedtime stories
when morning's shards

slice them into scrap?
Tonight we ate fresh eggs
for dinner, true dawn.
The laying hens? I'd eat *them* too,
my lips bleeding with their juices.

My screen glows in the dark
just like yours. When I pick
cherries, I pick the stem too,
just to throw it away later.
That's the only explanation I have

for dark wine, hard secrets.
A child is sighing in the next room,
a late request for explanation.
It begins to rain on all my misspelled
scenarios. Two dogs fight viciously

and everyone forgets. Even sin
is not so easily identified.
If we could be inoculated against it,
would we? One cloud drifts by
as if it has direction.

On our first flight,
my children were amazed
to watch the plane's wing
disappear, wondering
what held us aloft.

Once Upon a Time

I'm worried about cement. My life has come to this.
Cracks. Uneven settling. Gutter leak—*splat, splat.*
If I want to cry, I just read a children's book.
My kids leave home in two months.
We're throwing out the crayons! The cement guy lost
interest in the job. But he's a cement guy! He's not
supposed to lose interest! My tulips are spent,
sloppy green stalks and leaves flapping limp
against dirt. One of my students last week
dressed like the Pope from the waist up, naked
from the waist down. Exhibitionist tendencies
don't run in our family. We just say *fuck it*
and skip church. Do any of those books
really start, *Once upon a time*? At least I didn't pay
to have them jackhammer up the whole damn driveway,
put down perfect squares mocking future chaos.
I like living next to a bridge, here, on the edge
of Panther Hollow, as long as I know what's on
the other side. Once I threw pies during a public forum.
I remember their expressions right before *splat, splat.*
Maybe that's what we look like right before we die,
like, you're really not going to do that to me, are you?
I'm going to circle all the bad places in the driveway
with sidewalk chalk and hope it doesn't rain
and have a talk with John's Cement Repair, if John
actually shows up again. We never get our money's worth.
That's part of the deal. Do they teach that in college? Do I?
Speaking of which, bills. Speaking of which, hey, what
are we going to do with these extra beds? Have a sleepover?
Tell ghost stories to our adult friends? Be creative
with flashlights? Once upon a time, John did cement
repairs. He wore shin guards for kneeling. Maybe

I should have gotten down next to him and worshipped
at the shaved shrine. I took a cement pie to the face.
How much time do I have before it dries?
That's my question, scrawled for all to see—my neighbors
from upstairs windows, life-flight helicopters headed
to the hospital, even God, that surprising hot-air balloon,
rising up from the hollow.

TALKING ABOUT THE DAY

Each night after reading three books to my two children—
we each picked one—to unwind them into dreamland,
I'd turn off the light and sit between their beds
in the wide junk-shop rocker I'd reupholstered blue,
still feeling the close-reading warmth of their bodies beside me,
and ask them to talk about the day—*we did this,*
we did that, sometimes leading somewhere, sometimes
not, but always ending up at the happy ending of *now*.
Now, in still darkness, listening to their breath slow and ease
into sleep's regular rhythm.
                              Grown now, you might've guessed.
The past tense solid, unyielding, against the acidic drip
of recent years. But how it calmed us then, rewinding
the gentle loop, and in the trusting darkness, pressing play.

Model/Father

I separated the plastic pieces from their factory pressings
and carefully laid them out on the newspaper,
though I had not read it yet. I unfolded the thin
instructions and squinted and held them at a distance.
I blinked. Tab A into Slot B. I stuck a safety pin in the glue
to release it. I no longer needed a note from my father
to buy glue. I didn't sniff the glue. Not too much.
Not much at all, really.
                              I woke up eighteen years later—
my son had a beard, which he stroked semi-wisely,
and my daughter had breasts and a smirk I did not
recall. I compared my model to the one on the box.
Don't try this at home. Or on the road. Or anywhere.
I was missing a tiny piece—the brain, I think.
Directions are overrated. The father did not fit
in the bottle. The father emptied the bottle.
The father marked the bottle XXX. The father painted
the model, but his paintbrush was not tiny enough
for all the tiny parts. The model was a mess—
its mouth a slurred whisper, its belly thick
with layered paint. Its hair fell out due to a mysterious
lack of glue. We took it outside in the ice and snow.
My son brought the matches, my daughter the explosives.

ABOUT THE AUTHOR

Jim Daniels is the author of seventeen books of poetry. Daniels is also the author of numerous books of short stories, screenplays, and the editor of a number of anthologies. His poem "Factory Love" is displayed on the roof of a racecar, and two of his poems will be going to the moon soon. His poems have been featured on "Prairie Home Companion," Garrison Keillor's "Writer's Almanac," in Billy Collins' Poetry 180 anthologies, and Ted Kooser's "American Life in Poetry" series. A native of Detroit, Daniels is a graduate of Alma College and Bowling Green State University. He is the Thomas Stockham University Professor of English at Carnegie Mellon University.

www.ingramcontent.com/pod-product-compliance
Lightning Source LLC
Chambersburg PA
CBHW072045040426
42447CB00012BB/3028